DANNY SANDER

THE FRUIT GARDENER'S BIBLE

The Ultimate Guide on How to Grow Fruit Trees, Learn All the Valuable Information From Planning to Planting and Propagating Fruit-Bearing Trees

Descrierea CIP a Bibliotecii Naționale a României
DANNY SANDER
   THE FRUIT GARDENER'S BIBLE. The Ultimate Guide on How to Grow Fruit Trees, Learn All the Valuable Information From Planning to Planting and Propagating Fruit-Bearing Trees / Danny Sander – Bucharest: Editura My Ebook, 2021
   ISBN

DANNY SANDER

THE FRUIT GARDENER'S BIBLE

The Ultimate Guide on How to Grow Fruit Trees, Learn All the Valuable Information From Planning to Planting and Propagating Fruit-Bearing Trees

My Ebook Publishing House
Bucharest, 2021

TABLE OF CONTENTS

1 INTRODUCTION	7
2 FRUIT TREE FUNDAMENTALS	9
Basic Planning	9
Practical Matters	10
Plotting It Right	12
Special Note	14
3 FACTORING IN THE ENVIRONMENT	16
Light	16
Exposure	18
Frost Dates and Hardiness Zones	19
Soil	21
4 PURCHASING YOUR FRUIT TREE	23
Bare Rooted Stock	25
Balled And Burlapped Stock	25
Container Stock	26
Healthy Plants	26
Planting Your Trees	28
Planting Container Stock	29
Planting Bare Root Stock	30

Planting A Balled And Burlapped Root Stock 31
Tree Stakes And Supports ....…………… 32

**5 YOU'VE PLANTED THE TREE, NOW WHAT?
CARE OF FRUIT TREES** 34

Water ………………………………………….. 35
Mulch ……………………………………………….. 35
Feed …………………………………………………... 36
Weed …..………………………………………….….. 37
Pests And Diseases …………………………………... 38
Pest Control Systems …………………………....….. 40
Manual Controls …………………………………….. 40
Biological Controls …………………………………. 42
Chemical Controls …………………………………... 42

6 THE KINDEST CUT OF ALL – PRUNING ……... 44

Pruning Tools ……………………………….……….. 44
After Planting Pruning ……………………………… 46
Central Leader Pruning …………………………….. 46
Open Center Pruning ……………………………….. 47
Second And Third Year Pruning ……………...…….. 48
Pruning After The Fourth Year …………………….. 48
Cutting …..…………………………………………... 49

7 PROPAGATION ……………………………….…… 53

Grafting Methods ….…………………………..……. 55
Specific Methods ….…………………………..……. 56
Grafting Tools …………………………………..…... 57

CONCLUSION ……………………………………….. 59

1
INTRODUCTION

There are many compelling reasons why you might want to grow a fruit tree or trees in your front or back yard. Ideally, it is because you want to taste fruit fresh from the tree. There is nothing like the experience of biting into a freshly picked apple, cherry, peach or pear. You cannot beat a backyard fruit tree for freshness, availability and quality.

If you plant your own fruit tree, you have control over such things as variety. You can choose an unusual variety of fruit not usually found in the store. Stores tend to stick to the more popular or obvious choices. They may not stock heritage varieties. The store is also not responsible for the conditions in which the tree grows. You are. As a result, you can ensure the fruit trees are free from heavy use of pesticides, herbicides and other chemical products.

Another reason to grow your own fruit tree is the beauty and distinctiveness it can add to your garden. Trees are graceful and elegant or short and stocky. They are a natural force unto themselves. A fruit tree adds grace, beauty and shade. If you plant it in the right location, the tree will be a focal point, a specimen tree, a conversation topic.

Basically therefore, there are 3 very good reasons for planting a fruit tree in your garden. A fruit tree is a source of fresh and tasty food. It is a focal point. It also provides shade during the hot summer days. In other words, a fruit tree is a multi-purpose plant. In the following chapters, we will describe how you can grow fruit trees to achieve maximum benefit.

2
FRUIT TREE FUNDAMENTALS

BASIC PLANNING

When you decide to grow a fruit tree you need to carefully consider a variety of factors. The most important and immediate issue is your existing garden. Plants thrive best when they mesh well with their environment. As a result, you must never try to force the existing garden conditions into a form to match your "ideal" tree. You must pick the tree in accordance with the already existing environmental factors.

Admittedly, you can adjust such things as soil content, but you usually are unable to change such things as location, temperature, amount of light, frost dates, hardiness zone and size. Therefore, it makes perfect sense to pick a tree or variety suitable to the current conditions of your garden. This will ensure your fruit tree has a good chance of being healthier, easier to take care of and more productive. This makes perfect sense. Particularly when you know a healthy plant is less prone to diseases and other tree-specific pests. A healthy and happy tree will also tend to be more productive. It will produce more fruit for you and your family.

PRACTICAL MATTERS

Before you pick, let alone purchase your tree, you need to consider certain specific factors. These include chill factors, size accommodation, hardiness zone and use of the plant.

Chill Factors:

The chill factor refers to the amount of time the tree requires at low temperatures to break bud dormancy and grow in the spring. Some fruit trees are high-chill. This means they require more hours at temperatures below $44°$ F ($7°C$). High-chill fruit trees do not perform to their best potential in mild climates. Apples, in general, are a classic example of high chill fruit trees. Fortunately, there are medium and low chill trees as well. Granny Smith is a low chill variety of apple as is Braeburn. Bonita, Gold Dust and Sungold are low chill pears. Earligold, Garden Annie and Tilton are low chill apricots. Be sure to check the chill factors of the species and variety you want before you decide to purchase it.

Size Accommodation:

How big is your garden? Make sure you pick a fruit tree that fits into its allotted space. If the tree you want is too large, this will cause severe problems. Trees forced into confined spaces may become stressed. They will not perform or produce to their potential.

If you still want the specific tree, change the variety. Look for dwarf cultivars. Alternatively, consider a tree with compact growth habitat. Instead of a traditional apple, you could select a Colonnade Apple. It has short branches and grows about 10'.

Never ignore the size of your tree relative to that of your garden. If you do so, you will constantly have to prune. You will need to shape the tree. In doing so, you will also reduce the potential harvest of the tree through constant pruning.

Hardiness Zone:

It is imperative you know what zone your garden is in. If you do not, find out. Fruit trees, like all plants, have a specific hardiness. If you place a tropical tree in a lower number e.g. 1, 2 zone, it will not survive, let alone thrive. If you place an apple tree in a higher zone, it may also die. Be sure you match the fruit tree to the right zone. Also check for micro-environments. You may have a colder or warmer zone in your specific area than the norm.

Plant usage: What is the intent of the plant? Is it a foundation planting? Do you want it to act as the entryway to your garden? Maybe it is a specimen planting. Do you intend to place it on an informal lawn, slight slope or open area? Is its intended place the road allowance or curbside? Maybe you think it is best to put it in a container. All these possibilities can and will affect the type of tree you should select for your garden plot.

PLOTTING IT RIGHT

Once you know the basics, you need to plan your garden. Using graph paper or a computer program, sit down and sketch the existent garden. Note its structure and orientation. Mark on the garden "map" such things as shaded and sunny spots. You must know these factors if you are to decide what type of tree yopu can have and where to place it.

As well as the factors of sun and shade, you also need to note any exposed areas. Is there any spot in your garden where it is more open to the elements? Are their higher spots of land or any lower areas? Some sections, due to their height or lack of same, may be more susceptible to frost.

What are the light levels in your garden? Some gardens are only welcoming to plants with a high tolerance to sun or shade. Some have morning sun but lack afternoon or evening light. There are also gardens that are constantly affected by the building structures around them. Buildings may tower over certain sections, blocking out light for specific times of day. Other gardens may be entirely open to the elements, having no shelter at all.

Do not ignore the soil type or types in your garden sketch. Note what they are and include the pH levels. Be aware of the texture and the presence of organic and inorganic matter. Has the soil been treated? Does it need any type of enrichment? Is this the soil compatible with your favored fruit tree?

Note on your sketch other pertinent items such as frost dates, hardiness zones and any microclimates. Once you have all this data recorded, you can begin to talk about what tree and/or variety is the perfect match for your garden. First, however, you need to do more research on your specific environment. By understanding what factors may affect your fruit tree, you can educate yourself for making the right choice and prepare for dealing with the possible problems.

SPECIAL NOTE

One other factor you should consider in your plans and planting is fertility and fertilization. Keep in mind many fruit trees are **NOT** self pollinating. They require the presence of at least one other fruit tree to become fruit bearing. Check into the facts about tree pollination before you opt for your tree. This will indicate whether you have to have another tree or can have a single specimen.

Apricots and tart or sour cherries are self-pollinating. Plums, sweet cherries, apples, pears and African pears are not. While some cross-pollination trees may give you some fruit without a partner, they have a higher and better quality yield with another plum tree. It is best to provide them with a partner. These now companion trees must be within 100 feet of each other.

In selecting a companion tree, be aware of the basic facts of pollination. Not only will your fruit tree require another tree within bee range, but it will also need a different variety. In other words, if you want to have fruit on a McIntosh Tree, you have to have another variety, e.g. Red Delicious, to succeed. In some instances, you will have to have at least 2 other varieties in addition to your selected fruit tree. This is true of the pear tree. It is more difficult to fertilize.

It is hopeful you have bees in the area that make regular visits to your garden. They will initiate the fertilization process. If bees are on the decline due to the wind, insecticides or flower competition, there are alternatives. You can cross-pollinate on your own. Use a brush to dust the blossoms.

3
FACTORING IN THE ENVIRONMENT

The existent environment is an integral part of ensuring you can successfully grow a fruit tree. Environmental factors include light, exposure, frost dates, hardiness zones and soil. Each of these elements must be examined before you select a tree for your garden. If you do not select a tree suitable to your external environment, you will jeopardize your chance of growing a fruit tree to maturity and reaping the benefits of its fruitfulness.

LIGHT

Let it be perfectly clear. All fruit trees require sunshine to grow and fruit. Usually, they require lots of bright light. Most fruit trees demand a minimum of 8 hours a day during the summer. There are 4 basic categories of light. There is full sun with all its intensity. There is partial shade - part sun and part shade. There is also light shade and full shade. In general, fruit trees do not do well under full shade and light shade conditions. They prefer full sun, but some varieties will tolerate partial shade.

Remember, when gauging the amount of light in your yard, to consider other significant factors. You have to look at the following elements to determine the actual amount of light in your garden.

- **Time of year**

What is the amount of light you receive during the entire year? Look at each season as it affects the light in your garden. Determine the amount of light - particularly for the crucial periods of the year.

- **Location**

Where your garden is in terms of land formations, place and urban or rural situation will affect the amount of light you receive. For example, coastal regions may be mountainous. These obviously dictate different amounts and types of light than valleys or prairies.

- **Built environment**

Is your garden shaded by other structures? Does your house or a house next door cast a shadow at certain times of day? Is there an apartment building or office tower perpetually throwing your garden into the shade? Do not forget the impact of fences, walls and even sheds.

All these factors will have an effect upon the amount of light you will receive in your garden. The quantity of light affects the ability of your plant to reach its full growth and fruit bearing potential. If you have shade or shady areas, be sure to look at specific varieties that can tolerate this type of environment.

Note that apples might require cool autumn nights, but they need plenty of sunshine to produce their fruit. Fig trees need full sun as do peach trees, pears, plums, quince and cherry. Citrus, while liking full sun, can suffer from leaf scorch. As a result, during some periods of growth and development, cherry trees are better in partial shade.

EXPOSURE

Another facet to consider is exposure. As noted previously in reference to the lemon tree, full light is desirable, but blistering sun is counterproductive. It is essential you understand that such factors as the wind, salt spray and frost pockets can affect your tree. Is your garden open to these problems? Are you on a coastline? Does the wind blow through your garden like a tornado? Is your property subject to hurricanes? Do you get frost in your garden before anyone else?

Wind and heat are the most probable elements to cause damage to your fruit tree or trees. Frost and cold can affect their very survival. If your garden is susceptible to heavy or copious amounts of rain, it may also damage some types of fruit trees. Be aware of these possible problems. Try to correct what you can by erecting or removing barriers. Better yet, pick a tree suitable to those immutable conditions in your garden.

FROST DATES AND HARDINESS ZONES

Some fruit trees are more susceptible to frost than others. Cherries, for example, easily suffer frost damage to their blossom bud. Lemons can tolerate light frost while many varieties of apple tree are hardier. Peaches are probably the most susceptible trees in North America to blossom-kill by late frosts. In the northern parts of Canada, the United States and Europe, winter cold and frost damage create severe limitations to growing fruit trees. Be aware of the frost dates for your region. You will also need to know the hardiness zone.

Every country, region and even county has what is referred to as a hardiness zone. The hardier a plant, the more capable it is of surviving low temperatures. The higher the number of the hardiness zone, the warmer the range of temperatures. For example, if you live in zone 10, your plant needs to tolerate minimum temperatures of 30°F. Within zone 3, however, the minimum temperature is cited as –40°F.

To ensure your fruit tree will survive and thrive in the conditions of your garden, select the tree in accordance to the temperature range. Most apple trees, for example, are more tolerant of cold temperatures than are peach trees. Yet, within each group of plants, there are varieties capable of coping better than others. Some are more winter hardy than others.

Winter hardy peaches include Belle of Georgia, Oldmixon Free and Reliance. Winter hardy Apricots consist of Alfred, Godcot and Sungold, to name a few. If you are looking for hardy sweet cherries consider Gold, Rainier, Windsor and Yellow Glass. Cold hardy pears include Clapp's Favorite, Golden Spice and Lincoln. If you are in North America, you will find the Native varieties of plums are hardier than either the Japanese or European imports. Japanese plums are not only less hardy than the native or European types, but are more susceptible to frost. Most citrus fruit is not winter hardy.

In addition to the general zone, you may also have to look at the specific hardiness zone of your city or region. There are many micro-environments within the larger regions. Some of these may actually have a different hardiness zone. It may vary significantly enough to affect the choice of fruit tree.

SOIL

The type of soil you have in your garden is another factor in selecting the right fruit tree. The air, nutrients, water and organic matter that comprise it are vital to creating and maintaining healthy fruit trees. While sometimes you can alter the basic composition of the soil e.g. enrich it, replace it, add chemicals, it is often best to work with what you have. Avoid altering it in its entirety for the sake of your specific choice of plant. From the start, you need to know what type of soil you have in your garden.

Soils are usually described as sandy, clay or loam. Some fruit trees survive better in one type over another. In general, however, fruit trees prefer deep, well drained soil. This excludes sandy soils which do not hold water well. Clay soils, on the other hand, tend to retain water, sometimes too much water, becoming water logged. Loam soils are better than the other varieties. Yet, the best types of soil for fruit trees tend to be combinations - sandy loams and clay loams. These retain water and offer the right consistency of desirable qualities.

The productivity of soils is also determined by their acidity or alkalinity - the pH level. It influences the ability of the soil to make plant nutrients available. The pH scale ranges from 0 to 14. If it is less than 7, the soil is acidic. If the level is more than 7 the soil is alkaline. In general, fruit trees do best in soils that are slightly acidic to neutral. In other words, the soil is best if it as a pH level of 6.5 to 7.

Yet, whatever the acidity and type of soil, be sure to add organic matter. All soils benefit from the addition of these nutrients. When you mix in organic matter you improve the lightest and heaviest soil. You can buy organic materials for your garden as well as provide earthworms. In addition, you can start your own composting facility and add the material to increase your garden's fertility. Whether you purchase it or create it, be sure you combine both brown (dry) and green (fresh) organic matter together to create the right type of organic compost needed for the health of your fruit trees.

4

PURCHASING YOUR FRUIT TREE

Once you have figured out the essential elements of your garden environment, you can go ahead and select your fruit tree. You may opt for hardy and semi-hardy apple or cherry trees. You might also be able to plant and grow the more tender citrus and the fickle peach or pear. Whatever the specific tree you want, all types and varieties are referred to as "stock."

Within the stock available, you have the chance to select from 2 basic sorts. You may want "standard" stock or you could prefer dwarf stock. The former is the standard of the variety. It is the norm. It is the full size of any fruit tree if grown from a seedling. It is also the gauge against which you measure the rest and determine whether the tree is a dwarf variety. You need a ladder to pick the fruit from such a tree.

Dwarf stock is a tree of smaller size than typically produced by the average or normal seedling. Frequently, it is less than one-half the standard size. You can often pick the fruit off a dwarf fruit tree by standing on the ground. At most, you require a chair or small step ladder. A genetic dwarf grows naturally small in size as opposed to Banzai trees which are manually manipulated to become dwarves.

Dwarf trees can be created through grafting to a dwarf root stock, manipulating through pruning, breeding or through withholding certain required nutrients. In case you are not aware, the fruit of a dwarf tree are not smaller than those of the standard. A Red Delicious apple from a dwarf tree is identical in size to one from a standard Red Delicious tree. In large orchards and in small gardens, dwarf fruit trees tend to be the norm.

Whatever your favored type of tree and select size, you will find your next choice concerns the type of stock you will purchase. Nurseries and mail order plant companies usually sell trees in 3 basic formats. Trees come to you as bare rooted stock, balled or burlapped stock or container stock. Each type has its own advantages. Each also has its disadvantages. Some of these are economic; others are based on plant conditions. It is up to you to decide which stock you will purchase.

BARE ROOTED STOCK

Bare rooted stock is a descriptive term of the actuality of the product. Your fruit tree will come to you with its roots bared. They are surrounded only with moist sawdust. Alternatively, peat or sphagnum moss acts as a basic covering. The root stock can also be covered with a plastic wrapping. Whatever the type of protection provided, the root stock should be moist; the roots must appear healthy.

You usually order bare rooted stock through a mail order company. It is the least expensive of the options for purchasing a fruit tree. It can be bought ahead of time for spring planting. The tree is dug, shipped to you and bought just in time for a dormant planting.

BALLED AND BURLAPPED STOCK

You can also purchase your fruit tree as a ball and burlapped stock (B & B). Essentially, the fruit tree grower digs up the tree, leaving the soil around its roots. They wrap the roots around with a burlap bag and often a wire cage to protect them. The trees are field grown and are sold after they have reached a year old.

B & B stock are more expensive than bare rooted stock. They have the advantage of having the extra soil. You can also plant a B & B at any time during the season. Yet, there may also be a problem with the roots. When they are removed from the earth, some roots may be severed. This will require you take extra care after transplanting them to your garden.

CONTAINER STOCK

Another way you may obtain a fruit tree is to purchase it in a pot. Container stock comes in a pot with soil. It is usually a well-established tree. It is also easy to transplant. While it is the most expensive option of the 3 provided here, it is one of the best. The roots are usually intact and you can plant the tree any time. Examine the tree to make sure it is not pot or root bound - the roots having extended to the limits of the pot, using up all the soil. This is often visible. Look at the bottom of the container and see if any roots are escaping through the drainage holes.

HEALTHY PLANTS

Whatever form you decide to buy your tree in, you must make sure it is healthy. This may be a problem if you are purchasing your tree from a nursery catalogue. In this instance, try to order trees of no less than 1 year-old. Try to pick those that have trunks of ½ to ¾". An exception is a peach tree. These tend to have thicker stumps of ¾ to 1 ½". To ensure you are going to receive the best, check with other gardeners about the firm's reputation for delivering safe and healthy plants.

Never, ever purchase a plant that looks unhealthy. This is more difficult if you order your plant from a nursery catalogue. It is easier when you can you can actually go to a garden nursery or your local garden center. Here, you can examine the trees and look out for specific problems. If the tree has a weak stem or appears damaged, do not buy it. If its root is dry and withered. Do not buy this fruit tree. Even if they offer you a good "deal" or it is free do not take this tree home.

You must be selective when you pick the root stock for your tree. Stop and take the time to check out all the parts visible. Be sure to read up on the subject before you go. Know what a healthy pear, citrus, peach, apple or plum looks like. Buy from a reputable nursery or other seller. If possible, make sure you can return the plant if it exhibits serious problems or defects.

When you are looking at the plant, consider the following as a basic guideline to purchasing a healthy fruit tree.

- Make sure the tree, dwarf or standard stock, is compact. If it is leggy, it has probably been deprived of light.
- Check out the color of the plant. Make sure it exhibits healthy buds. There should be no dead or dying vegetation.

- Examine the leaves for any sort of damage. This could be from insects, fungi or disease.
- Look closely at the leaf and flower buds. If when you touch the tree, they fall off easily, it may indicate the tree has been deprived of water.
- Touch and gently bend the stems. They need to be supple, strong and unbroken.
- Look at the leaders - the shoots that spring from the main branch. They must also be strong.
- Take a look at the bark of the fruit tree. It must have no nicks, cuts or any other type of damage. Cuts in the bark can make some fruit trees more easily accessible to diseases and various types of fungal infections.
- Examine the root balls. They must be soft and moist. Root balls must never be dry.
- If the stock is in a container, see if it is root or pot bound. If it is, do not buy this fruit tree. Pot bound trees have a tendency to not thrive.

PLANTING YOUR TREES

After you have selected your root stock and brought it home, you will need to plant it. The method to establishing the fruit tree properly is similar for all 3 types of tree stock. There are, however, variations you need to consider. This is particularly true for specific fruit trees. Below, you will find a generalized planting method for each root stock. For further information on the planting of certain varieties, talk to the nursery and/or consult experts in the area.

PLANTING CONTAINER STOCK

Start by digging a hole. It must be at least twice the size of the pot. Turn the pot upside down to release the tree. Do not tug or pull to do so. This might damage the stock and scion. Only empty the pot just prior to planting.

Do not simply stick the plant into the ground. Gently spread the roots out. Loosen them, freeing them to help the plant grow in the right direction. If necessary, score the roots if they have become densely wound around the bottom of the plant. If the roots are a solid mass at the bottom of the container, remove the affected ones. They are only going to hinder the growth of the young shoots.

Once the root stock is ready, have someone help you place the tree in the ground. Make sure it is at the same level as it stood in the pot. You might want to place it a little higher. This will give the soil room to settle.

When the plant is firmly inside the hole, cover the soil around it. Water it thoroughly. You might want to ensure it retains water by preparing a trench around it. This will help the water remain where it needs to be. To further help water retention and fertilization, fill in the trench with mulch.

PLANTING BARE ROOT STOCK

Before you plant bare root stock, you will need to soak the root system in water for 12 hours. During the last hours it is soaking begin to dig the hole. Make sure you dig a hole large enough to contain the roots and a section to allow expansion. You can start by digging the hole large enough to accommodate the root system without twisting.

If you can, have someone help you plant the trees. If this is not possible, prepare a handy tree support. You do this by tying 2 strips of wood together in such a manner as they form a fulcrum spanning over the hole. You then will tie the tree to the poles at the desired height. This apparatus will then hold the tree for you while you dig further and/or place the soil correctly around it.

Make sure you have a raised mound in the center of your hole for the tree to sit upon. You must have a larger hole around it. This allows for the roots to grow. Place the tree on the center mound so it is approximately 2" higher than it grew in the nursery. The old soil line from the nursery growth will be seen on the bark.

Make sure the tree is in the center and spread out the roots evenly. You can trim back any excessively long side roots. Be sure you place the lowest branches towards the southwest to help shelter the tree. If it is a windy site, tip the tree into the prevailing wind at about 3 to 5 degrees.

Refill the hole gently. You can either settle the soil with water as you go or wait until you have finished backfilling. Tamp the soil down with the heel of your foot. This will help to remove any large pockets of air.

About 2" from the tree build a shallow trench or dike. This will help the tree retain water. You can then fill the dike with mulch such as organic compost, leaves or straw. This further enhances the ability of the soil to keep in moisture and nutrients. You can then gently water the tree until the soil is well soaked.

PLANTING A BALLED AND BURLAPPED ROOT STOCK

When you dig the hole for this type of root stock, make sure the hole is twice the width of the root ball. Prepare the tree by removing the wire or wire basket before you plant. Removing the wire now, and the burlap later will allow the tree roots to have maximum contact with the soil immediately. In this way the roots do not become compacted.

Dig the hole so there is a central mound in the middle. This is where you will place the tree. You might have to roll the tree into the hole. Help is often essential when you have a B & B root stock to plant. Once the tree is in place, remove the burlap. Cut it away if necessary. Do so without harming the roots.

Begin to refill the hole and tree well. Gently pack the soil around. Dig a trench as noted above. Water the plant and move on to the next tree. After you have finished, consider whether you will need to stake the tree.

TREE STAKES AND SUPPORTS

Some fruit trees require support. This should be implemented as soon as possible after planting. Small trees make do best with a 2 stake method while larger varieties may require the 3 stake method. Stakes are used to help the trees grow and establish a solid root system in a particularly windy or exposed area.

All stakes are driven into the soil outside of the planting region. If you stake too close to the tree, you risk damaging the roots system. It will also prevent strong support. In the 2-stake system, drive 1 wooden stake on 1 side of the tree and the second stake on the other side. Run cable, rope, string or wire from the stakes to around the tree.

The 3 stake method uses 3 stakes, usually smaller metal pegs. Drive them sufficiently far from the tree, spreading them in a triangular fashion around the tree. Run from them cable, rope, string or wire to the tree. Attach these "ropes" to, but not directly on, the tree.

Use rubber hose or some other material to attach any of the materials to the fruit tree. This is applicable to both methods of staking. This will prevent harm to the bark. In either instance, give the tree some slack. You need to give the trees room to move in the wind. This allows them to build up the strength in their roots and bark as well as to adjust to the prevailing wind of the region.

Your tree is now planted and staked. Leave the staking in for about the first year of the tree's life. Now it is up to you to take care of the trees basic needs. We will discuss these in the next chapter. You may also need to prune the tree. You can find this information in the chapter titled *The Kindest Cut of All – Pruning*.

5
YOU'VE PLANTED THE TREE, NOW WHAT? CARE OF FRUIT TREES

Once your tree is firmly planted and staked, you cannot simply walk away and let nature take its course. You need to attend to the tree's needs on a regular basis. This includes watering, mulching, feeding, weeding and battling pests. While the care of the tree varies over its growing years, you still will have to watch the performance. If you do not establish a routine at the beginning of the tree's life in your garden, you may negatively affect its value.

You do need to watch how your tree grows. If you want a healthy tree, free from pests and diseases, you need to make sure you give it the right start in life. Only then can your fruit tree reach its full potential.

WATER

Water is a very important ingredient in your tree's diet. It is responsible for refreshing it as well as ensuring the nutrients in the soil reach the roots for absorption. Water also helps the tree absorb the nutrients. Water is especially important for your newly transplanted tree.

You will need to water the fruit tree regularly for the first season of its life in your garden. This means a weekly dose of water. It also means a deep watering. You are not helping the tree if all your do is water the surface. A frequent surface watering is actually counterproductive. It does not help the plant establish itself.

A deep, slow, infrequent watering is good for the tree's development. It encourages the growth of a stronger root system. It adapts the tree to seeking out the water trapped deep in the soil. Once you establish a strong root system, you do not need to water the tree as frequently.

MULCH

No matter how old the tree is, mulching the soil around it is beneficial. Choose organic material whenever possible. This can include leaves, compost and/or straw. Place it about 5-10 cm

(2-4") thick around the tree base. Do not pile it against the actual trunk of the tree. If it is too close to the actual tree trunk, the mulch may trap moisture prohibiting air circulation. This could result in fungal-related problems.

Mulching serves 3 purposes. First, it helps the soil retain moisture. Second, it provides vital nutrients. Third, mulching helps keep the weeds away. All 3 functions are critical during the first year of your fruit tree. At the same time, mulching also saves you work while establishing a healthy pattern of care and responsibility. Remember to replenish the mulch as it breaks down.

FEED

It is important that you feed or enrich the soil. At the very least, feeding the soil maintains its health. Depending upon your philosophy, and the by-laws of your community, you have a number of choices. Essentially, the "meals" of your fruit tree can be either organic or chemical. The form they may take may be liquid, water-soluble powder, slow-release pellets or granules or bulk material. It will be up to you, in consultation with experts in the area, which you prefer to work with.

Organic matter is popular among many fruit tree growers. Within the various types of organic matter, you can find simple or complex combinations. Animal manure is the simplest.

Others combine egg shells with animal manure and various types of meal e.g. bone, kelp or blood. Organic fertilizers may be alfalfa pellets, corn gluten, bat guano, leaf mold, crushed oyster shells, glacial rock dust, green sand, earthworm casting and mycorrhizal fungus. You can compost your own fertilizer or purchase it. Be aware that some of the organic material can be smelly and may attract urban wildlife.

If you choose chemicals, be sure you check it out with a nursery first. Read the labels for application. You may also want to see whether the law in your region permits application of certain substances. Be sure you know how much your soil requires. If it is not deficient in nitrogen do not apply formulae with high amounts.

The same is true for the other basic nutrients your fruit tree needs: phosphorus and potassium. Your fruit tree also requires such trace or secondary elements as calcium, magnesium and sulfur in smaller quantities than the primary nutrients. If you apply too much, you are in danger of harming your fruit trees. Excessive amounts of even the trace elements can poison your tree.

WEED

Weeds in any garden are a pest. They take away vital nutrients. They compete for space and light. Weeds may also bring in fungi and diseases. While mulching may help keep down the weeds, it is not always successful. You will need to personally bend down and pull them out. Begin the process when both your tree and the weeds are young and small.

There are many reasons to remove weeds at their early stage. Small weeds are easier to remove. You can dig up a tuber root quicker before it develops into a deep, firmly entrenched system. Smaller weeds are not at the point of becoming entwined systems of mass production. You can nip off their ability to reproduce through seeds or underground runners. This will slow down weed production for the next season as well.

PESTS AND DISEASES

Trees are subject to a variety of pests and diseases. Some trees are more susceptible to specific problems than others. Both apple trees and pears are subject to coddling moth while cherries suffer from the cherry fruit fly. Birds are a common enough pest. Other insects causing trouble are aphids and wasps. Some insects, like diseases are tree specific. You will need to read about possible problems. Talk to the experts at your nursery or garden store. Check up on the internet and look up various agricultural sites and send away for or download pamphlets on the topic.

There are also ways to help decrease the possible effects of pests and diseases.

- Buy only healthy plants.
- Opt for highly resistant varieties. Jonathan apple trees, for example are highly resistant (HR) to scab but susceptible to mildew while Liberty apple trees are HR to scab, apple rust and fireblight. Fireblight also affects Pears. The Kieffer, Lincoln, Moonglow and Warren varieties are resistant to his problem. Indian Free Peach and Loring Peach are leaf curl resistant varieties.
- Be sure you feed, water and keep your tree healthy. Healthy trees have higher resistance to disease and pests than their unhealthy counterparts.
- Keep your soil healthy. If you provide the right nutrients and prevent incursion of weeds and disease carrying plants, your fruit tree has a better chance of remaining healthy.
- Avoid stressing your plants out. Trees need spacing and air circulation. If they have to compete for nutrients, air and water, they become stressed. This weakens their resistance opening them up for a variety of problems.

PEST CONTROL SYSTEMS

There are different ways to control pests. As with providing fertilizers, you have the choice of chemical and more natural forms of addressing the issues. Again, it is a matter of local legislation or even by-laws as well as personal preference. Always be sure to consider the options and the effects your choice may have not only on your fruit tree but on the total environment.

MANUAL CONTROLS

This option is labor intensive. It depends upon your willingness to spend time picking off such things as insects by hand. It is best implemented at the very beginning of the problem - before it becomes an actual infestation. Sometimes, you may have to lop off or remove diseased or infested parts. You could also set traps to catch the insects. Setting up bird warnings, scarecrows, banging pans or other methods of chasing away birds is also manual control measures.

One of the most common methods of scaring birds away is to create a "Scare Eye." This is an aluminum pie plate or a strip of foil. You hang these devices in the tree. The noise and motion scares the birds away. Be careful, however, birds may learn that the eyes are more noise than substance.

Another option is to place netting over the tree prior to the ripening of the fruit. This is one of the most effective deterrents to fruit loss. While cumbersome if you have a large orchard, it is manageable if you have no more than 2 or 3 fruit trees. Netting is quite popular for cherry, peach and plum trees.

Rodents e.g. mice, voles, rabbits often cause damage during the winter. There is a simple way to prevent this. You go to your garden supply store. Ask for and purchase coiled plastic guards. You can install these shortly after you plant the tree. They are durable and expand with the growth of the tree. Read the instructions carefully before you begin to wrap the coil around the tree. Do use gloves.

Insects, too, can be treated or handled manually. You may pick off insects from the branches, leaves and twigs. You can also burn tent caterpillar nests. Remove by hand evidences of harmful varieties of larvae before they mature and become insect infestations. To understand the insect life cycle, read up on it. Be able to recognize the various stages. Know how to identify harmful varieties of pests. You do not want to eradicate the good with the bad.

BIOLOGICAL CONTROLS

Biological controls usually come into play in treating a problem with insects. This form of pest management involves using natural predators. This means birds, frogs, spiders, lady bugs/beetles and even certain types of bacteria. Among the beneficial insects for fruit trees, you will find the Ladybug Beetle, the Lacewing and the Syrphid fly. Ladybugs prey on aphids, scale and mites. Lacewings attack aphids, leafhoppers, mites, scales and specific moth eggs e.g. Oriental Fruit Moths. The Syrphid Fly eats aphids and scale. You will need to create an environment attractive to beneficial insects or birds. While attracting birds when you have a cherry tree may seem counterproductive, it may actually be beneficial in the long run when it prevents other more serious problems with insects.

CHEMICAL CONTROLS

Many individuals consider chemicals the last resort. The major problem with using chemicals is their inability to differentiate between beneficial insects and bacteria and bad ones. You may actually cause more harm than good by spraying. If you feel you really have to use chemicals on your fruit trees, try to go organic. There are many different organic solutions at your local garden center.

Before you spray, talk to people who know all the alternatives. Do your research. Better still, consider prevention. I cannot stress it enough. A healthy, well fed and cared for tree is far less vulnerable to diseases and pests than weaker, neglected plants.

6
THE KINDEST CUT OF ALL – PRUNING

Pruning is a necessary fact of owning fruit trees. You will have to prune them to provide the tree with the best means of producing fruit. Essentially, pruning gives the tree shape and direction. It open it up to allow access to light and air. According to some experts, pruning is the most essential maintenance task you will have. It is also the easiest to mess up. You may want to read up on the subject, including theories on when and how to prune. There are also courses you can take. Do talk to experts and look into courses offered locally. There are on-line sources to consider and local tree nurseries may be able to offer some guidance.

PRUNING TOOLS

Yet, no matter how good a learner you are, you will need to make sure you have the best help on hand. In order to prune correctly, you will need specific tools. They include:

- Secateurs
- Loppers
- pruning saws
- pole saws
- long-reach pruners
- ladder
- gloves

In selecting your pruning tools, be sure they are capable of pruning fruit trees. Dollar store tools may well be able to handle cut flowers, but are usually not capable of trimming branches. Pruning saws, for example, are designed with teeth specifically made to cut through green wood. The ladder may be generic. If you have dwarf trees you will not likely require it.

In addition to these tools, you will also be able to employ your thumbs for pinching. Your thumb and forefinger can also do de-budding. An alternative is to employ a small knife. Make sure all tools are kept in good repair, sharp and ready for work.

Take good care of all your pruning tools. Wear gloves to protect your hands. Be sure to wash your hands and your tools. Tools can carry diseases. Be sure to sterilize them. This will prevent you passing on any type of unwanted problem from fruit tree to fruit tree.

There are two theories in pruning. One states you must prune the tree as soon as you plant it. The other says no pruning during the first year. Consult with your nursery before you decide which to approach. Weigh any pros and cons for the effect upon your tree. Below are provided the different methods of pruning to give you some idea of the approaches to pruning a tree. Note specific trees require certain types of pruning. You will need to direct your approach to suit your type of fruit tree.

AFTER PLANTING PRUNING

There are 2 different methods of pruning just-planted fruit trees. One applies to apple, cherry and pear trees. This is the Central Leader or Modified Leader method. The other method is called the Open Center. It is applied to nectarines, peaches and plum trees.

CENTRAL LEADER PRUNING

Central Leader Pruning requires you to remove all the side branches from the tree. In the case of apple, sweet cherry and pear, you must cut the branches to the central leader (trunk) with a high cut just above the healthy vegetative bud. If you have a tart cherry tree, do not cut back as severe. This is called whipping the tree. The tree will end up at about 2.5' above the ground. It will resemble a central stem with all the scaffolding branches removed.

OPEN CENTER PRUNING

The open center system requires you to cut the trunk back to between 24 - 36". You must then select 3 long scaffold branches about 6" apart. Choose, if possible, the top branch that is growing into the wind. Next, trim the selected primary or scaffold branches running from the tree trunk to form a main structure of a canopy. Cut them back to having 2 buds each. The resultant tree will be truncated with 2 side branches and one off-center topper.

Both methods of pruning seem radical. At first glance, it would appear you are leaving a mere twig behind. In the end, however, you will be shaping the tree. You are also opening it up. In doing so, you are providing it with the best possible growth pattern.

The other approach to pruning assumes the basic pruning has already been accomplished at the nursery or garden center. It also takes for granted you will not need to do any serious pruning during the first year of growth. The only pruning you must do is the removal of dead branches. It is during the following year you take up the pruning shears and saws to create form.

SECOND AND THIRD YEAR PRUNING

Second year pruning takes place after the coldest weather has blasted through. It can also occur if you are planting a fruit tree more than a year old. This is a modified central leader system. It involves you taking your pruning shears or clippers and removing most of the branches.

You will clip off all the branches except for 3 or 4 well-spaced scaffolding branches. These will be spaced along the trunk some 6 to 8" apart. They will be scaffolds with wide not narrow angles. You will trim the leader branch to about a foot above where the desired next set of scaffolds will grow.

Third year pruning mimics the process of the second year. The basic spiral shape of the tree is well under way. During the fourth year, if it seems necessary, you can cut back further to increase the number of scaffold branches to 6 or even 8.

PRUNING AFTER THE FOURTH YEAR

Every year, be ready to snip off many of the scaffold branches. Always remove the thin and weak branches growing out from the scaffold branches. Always remove branches growing at awkward angles - sideways or upwards from the scaffolding. Watch your spacing. Be sure the central trunk is receiving light and air.

One basic principle of pruning is to try to keep the branches horizontal. This provides them with the strength to carry the weight of the fruit. You need to train them or remove the branches. This also prevents problems with wintering - crotch injury. Prune out the branches with narrower crotches and try to keep the branches horizontal. Always aim to retain branches with no less than a 35 degree angle.

To cut down on damaging or stressing the tree, keep on top of your pruning. Use common sense. A large branch is harder to cut off than a smaller one. A larger branch can also cause disruption. Light pruning is preferable. Heavy pruning alters the percentage of roots to foliage. This will disrupt such things as fruiting.

CUTTING

There are many different types of cuts you can use when pruning your fruit tree. Below are 4 basic types:

- **Cut back to the bud**

This is used on branches to redirect the growth. It also helps the branch to maintain a specific size. You cut the branch to about ¼" (0.5 cm) above the targeted bud. Be careful. You must make the cut to direct the branch in the way you want the tree to grow. You also need to realize that if you prune too far away from the bud or too close, the branch may fail to heal properly.

- **Lateral branch cut**

This allows you to shorten the limbs of a tree. It is made to redirect growth. You always cut at an angle. Never slice to close to the trunk, but do not leave a nub sticking out, either.

- **Removing limbs**

to do this you have to cut in a critical place. It ensures quick healing if you do so correctly. Do not slice all at once. When removing a limb approach the cut in steps. This will avoid damaging the bark. First cut 12-18" (30-45 cm) from the branch collar and about ⅓ through the branch. The 2nd cut is a bit further along and made from the top. The 3rd and final cut is just above the branch collar.

- **Thinning**

You thin to remove excess growth. This includes fruit, branches, stems and suckers. This is a term used in pruning to apply to a variety of cuts. You thin to remove excess growth. This includes fruit, branches, stems and suckers. You thin out branches to ensure there are no incorrectly growing branches on the fruit tree e.g crooked, crossing, vertical. It is also the removal of weaker stock. You remove the branches, stems or suckers in such a manner as to prevent further growth in that particular position on the tree.

People thin fruit to help the tree produce healthier and larger fruit. Although a tree thins itself out naturally, you can remove more of the developing fruit to produce a larger and tastier crop. Thin out the tiny fruitlets of apples and peaches soon after they set. This may mean you pinch the fruitlets off right after your fruit tree comes into bloom. You can remove some of the fruit then wait until the tree thins itself before deciding whether to remove more. You can also wait until after your tree thins itself before removing the unwanted or excess fruit. Whatever approach you adopt, do thin selectively. Only thin out the smallest, weakest, deformed and diseased fruitlets. Some fruits, such as cherries, however, require no thinning.

Pruning is an art and a science. You need to have the right tools. You also need patience and an understanding of what is best for the tree. You can choose to not prune. It will not actually harm your tree in any fashion. Such neglect will also not help your tree realize its full potential. Benignly not pruning can create some health issues. It will also insure your tree does not come to reach its full fruitfulness. While the decision is ultimately yours, it is strongly suggested you do prune. Learn how to do so and you may even come to enjoy the shaping and forming of the tree in your garden.

7
PROPAGATION

Fruit tree propagation is not for everyone. In fact, many choose not to. They leave it to the experts. This is because fruit tree propagation is not simply the planting of a single seed. It means you have to understand the reproductive system called grafting. The process will involve the union through forced means of two different plants: the scion or select part of the tree to be grafted to the stock.

The scion is the desired fruit bearing section (cultivar) of the tree. The stock is the host. It is in more senses than one - the base. It is the root system used to support the scion's growth and creation. At its very basics, grafting or budding is the attachment of the scion to the stock to produce a specific fruit tree. The stock also determines the mature size of the tree and, to an extent, the hardiness of the fruit tree. Some fruit growers will graft a more tender fruit tree onto a hardier stock.

Knowledge of grafting comes in handy in several ways. As noted previously, it is for propagation. It is also used to repair damage trees. During the winter, many fruit trees become damaged by frost, cold and rodents. If the upper branches are alive and trying to thrive, you can save the tree by using the live sections as scions for grafting. This is a specific type of grafting called bridge grafting.

Grafting is also employed to help a producer obtain several different cultivars (varieties) on the same tree. In some instances, a fruit grower has had more than 40 different types of cultivars producing fruit on the same tree. This is an extreme case. It is not highly recommended. While having more than one fruit on the same root stock sounds ideal, it can lead to dominancy problems. If kept under control, however, having more than one compatible cultivar on the stock root can make the process of cross pollination easier.

In selecting the host or stock for the scion in either cases, you must select a close botanical cousin. In bridge grafting, both scion and stock will be the original tree as it is a means of reviving it. In other forms of grafting, the stock is the root of a compatible variety. No matter what you hear, stone trees such as peach and plums will not grow on an apple or pome stock. The same applies to pome scions and stone root stock. However, you can grow different varieties of the same fruit on a tree. In doing so, you must take care to not affect the possible pollination process. As noted earlier, most fruit trees are not self-pollinated. They rely on another tree to pollinate them. If you combine antagonistic fruit trees, you may end up with little fruit.

Selecting the right type of root stock also affects the size of the mature tree. Dwarf root stock results in the creation of a dwarf tree. If you choose standard root stock, even though the dwarf tree is the scion, it will throw a normal size tree. Think ahead.

GRAFTING METHODS

There are many different methods you can employ when grafting your fruit trees. The choice depends upon a variety of factors. They include the specific tree you wish to graft and the geographical area you reside and grow your tree in. The specific advice you obtain from an experienced grafter in your region and any course you can take in grafting are also influential in how you graft.

By all means, do take the advice of the experts available in your own locality. They can provide you with pertinent information not available in general books or non-specific online sites. But do not stop there. If you can, do take a course on grafting. Sign up for a hands-on grafting class. It will be more helpful than reading. Reading books on the subject and from accurate online sources is helpful, but taking a course with a practical component is superior and more helpful in the long and short run.

SPECIFIC METHODS

The object of grafting is a specific type of fruit tree. In order to do so, you have to unite the cambium layer (which resides under the bark) of both the stock and the scion. This is another reason why the stock and scion require close botanical ties. Several means are at your disposal to accomplish this. Some are designed to address or correct a specific issue. The 3 major types are bridge, bud, cleft and root stock.

•**Bridge Grafting** involves using twigs of the top of the tree as the scion. They are inserted under the bark of the stock below the damaged area of the winter or animal ravaged tree. This is done to unify the cambium of the layers of the two: host and scion. If done properly, the sap will pass through the scions. The twigs will then grow and become incorporated into the tree. The dead wood is removed, the new tree pruned into shape.

• **Budding** takes the bud of a tree and uses it as the scion. The bud must be dormant. The sample must also contain the surrounding tissue if the scion and the stock are to combine their cambium. When the bud becomes established, you cut off the branch on which it sits to the bud. You also remove any competitive buds surround the scion.

• **Cleft Grafting** requires you cut a branch on the host tree into a square. You will leave a cleft. You then take a scion or more and insert it into the cleft in the stub of a branch.

• **Root Stock Grafting** is grafting for propagation. Usually this occurs in a nursery. The fruit trees you buy are generally already grafted. A scion of a branch is grafted to the root stock. The root stock is chosen for its hardiness and its ability to determine the size. The scion is selected to provide the best tasting fruit. Sometimes the root stock if left to develop would produce little or poor quality fruit. Combined with the scion, however, it is the producer of sweet and high quality produce.

GRAFTING TOOLS

A sharp knife is always required for grafting. What you also need is grafting tape. This holds the scion in whatever shape, to the host or stock. You can substitute any other type of adhesive tape including masking, electrical or duct. You can even use plastic strips to hold a bud or twig in place. Each of the alternatives can prevent a problem. Masking tape may unravel. Plastic strips may not co-operate well in trying to attach the bud in place. In the case of electrical or duct tape, you will need to slit them open after the graft proves successful. This will prevent impairment to the growth process.

If you only have a tree or 2, chances are you may never graft for propagation purposes. It may become handy, however, if you ever have trees that suffer from damage. For some individuals, grafting becomes a hobby as they find ways to provide new varieties on an old tree.

CONCLUSION

Owning a fruit tree is not as simple as having a vegetable or flower garden. If you want to have more than another pretty tree, you will have to understand the science of fruit trees. The logistics of planting, growing, maturing, pollinating and reproduction are more complex than the average annual or perennial plant. Trees require a thorough knowledge of their life cycle if you want to make them into productive or, rather, fruitful inhabitants of your garden.

Fruit trees are made for providing shade and shelter. They are also for supplying you, your family and friends with fruit. How bountiful the crop may be is up to you. From the beginning, you must determine the rightness of everything. You have to ascertain the correct type of tree. It must be one in harmony with the natural and built environment of your garden site. You cannot force the tree of your choice to thrive if it is not in synch with the soil, water, frost, shade, light and other aspects of the plot of land. Placed in an alien environment, your tree will have trouble surviving let alone thriving.

As a result, you need to consider all the aspects that will affect the growth of your tree. From the size of the plot, to the size of the tree, to the soil content, to pest resistance, to pruning demands to even propagation - all are part of the basics behind purchasing a tree. If you choose it wisely - after research and much study of local and regional factors, the tree will grace your garden with its beauty, its grace and its bounty.

www.ingramcontent.com/pod-product-compliance
Ingram Content Group UK Ltd.
Pitfield, Milton Keynes, MK11 3LW, UK
UKHW022213230426
12048UKWH00016BA/815